Learn How To Draw Animal Tattoos

Animal Tattoos Drawing Tutorial

Animal Tattoo

By : Gala Publication

2

Published By :

Gala Publication
© Copyright 2015 – Gala Publication

ISBN-13: **978-1522707219**
ISBN-10: **1522707212**

Table of Contents

4

SCORPION TATTOO

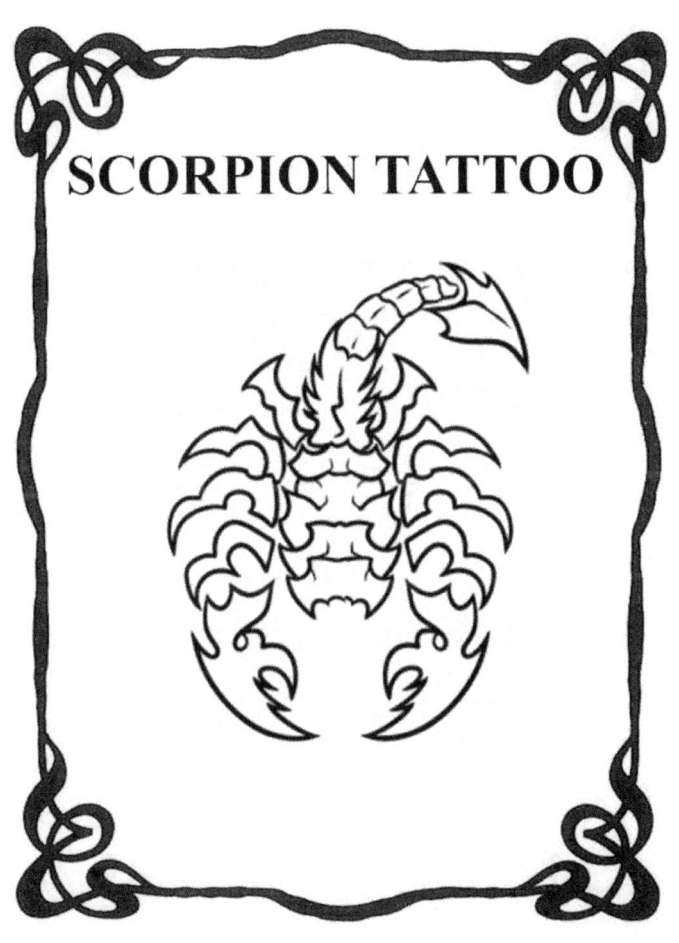

STEP 1

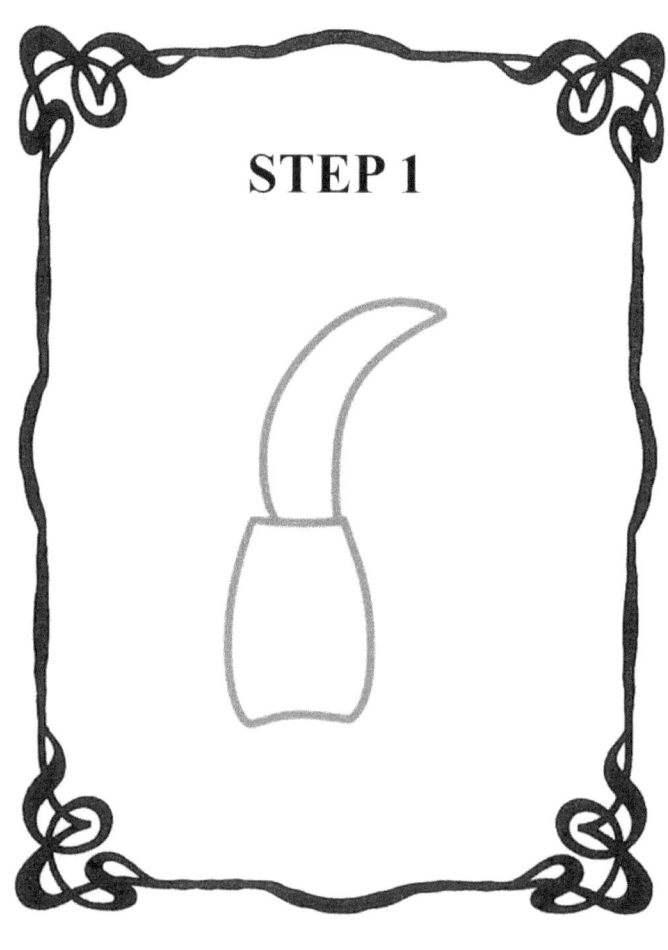

STEP 2

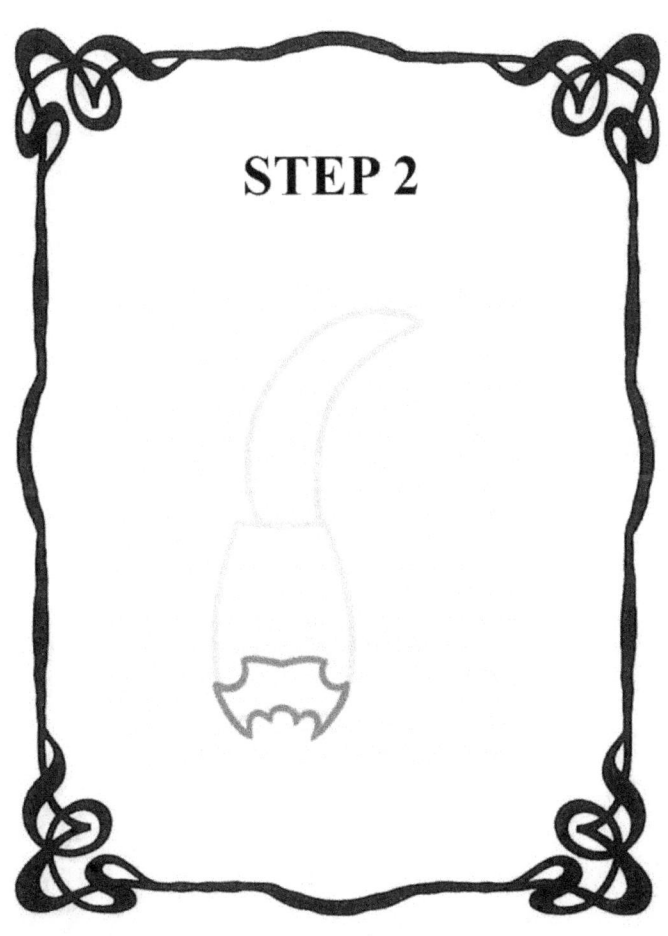

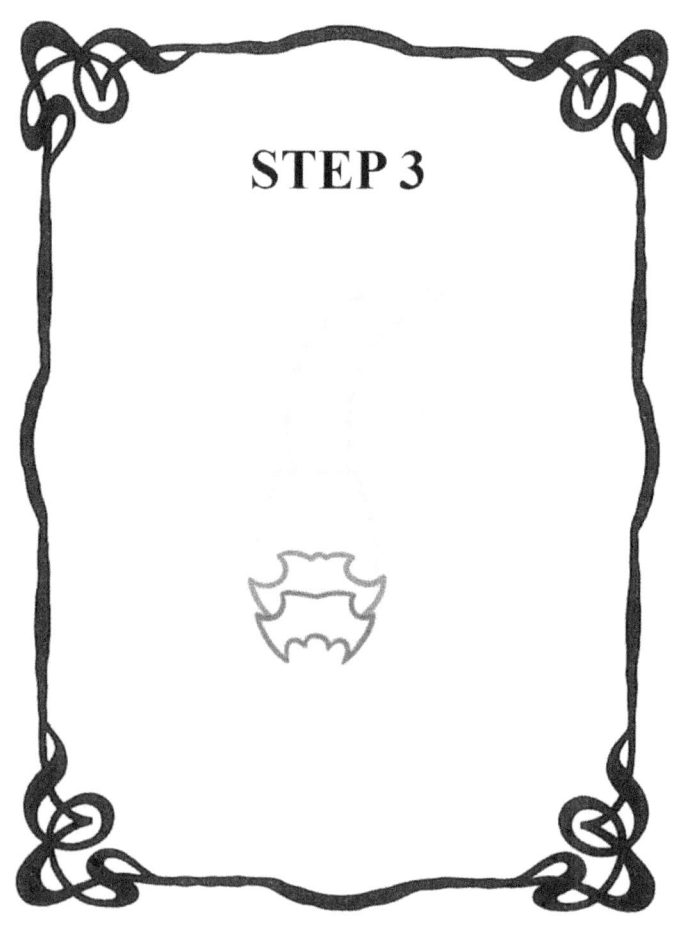

STEP 3

STEP 4

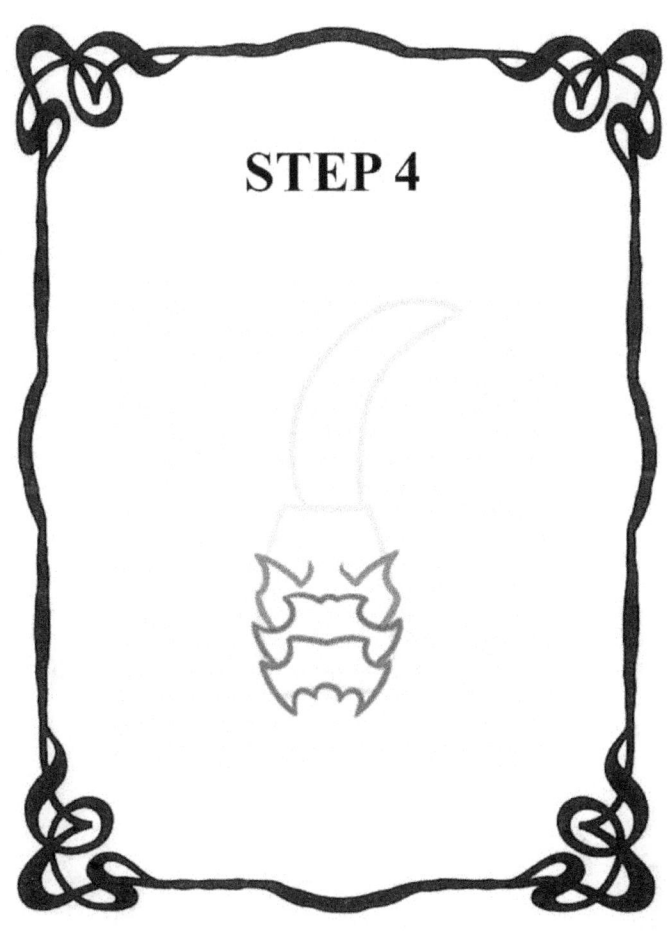

STEP 5

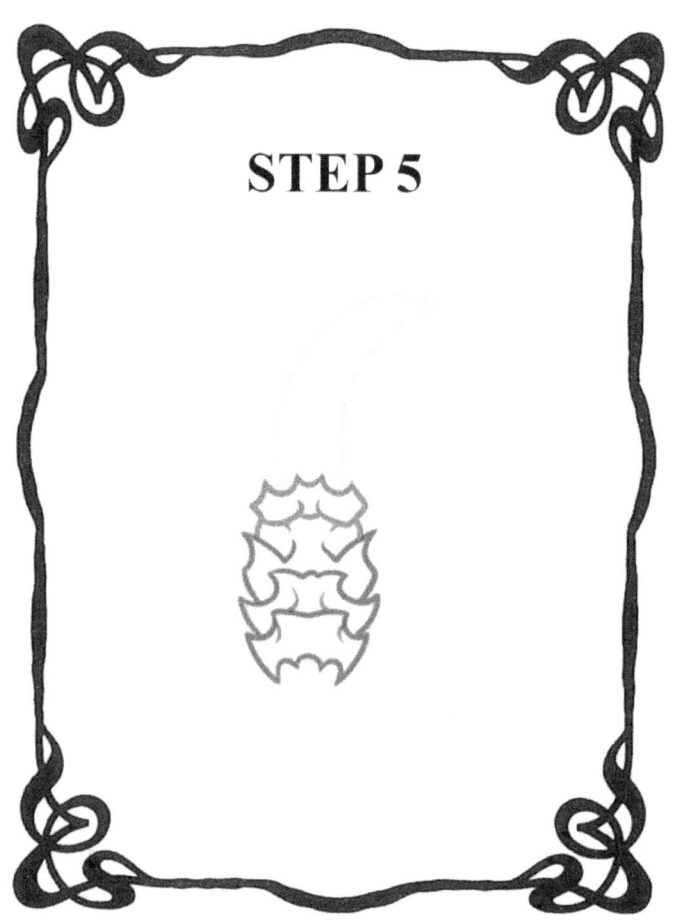

STEP 6

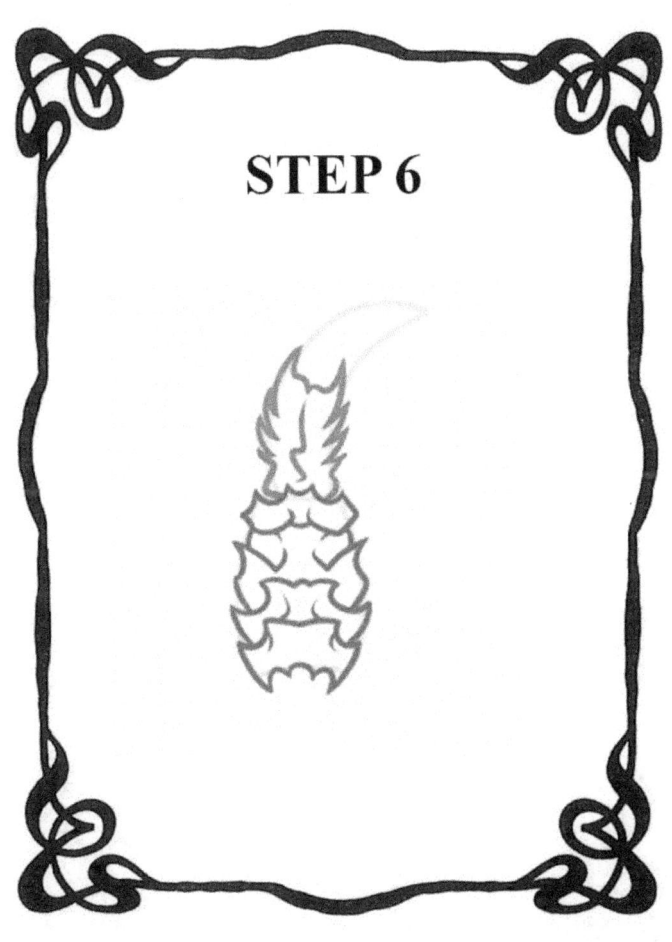

STEP 7

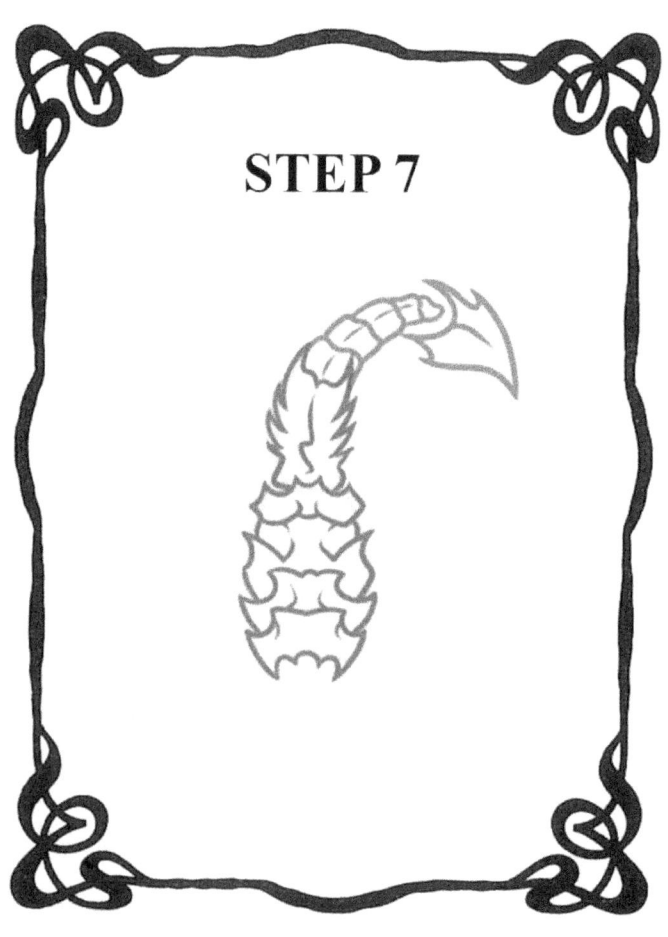

STEP 8

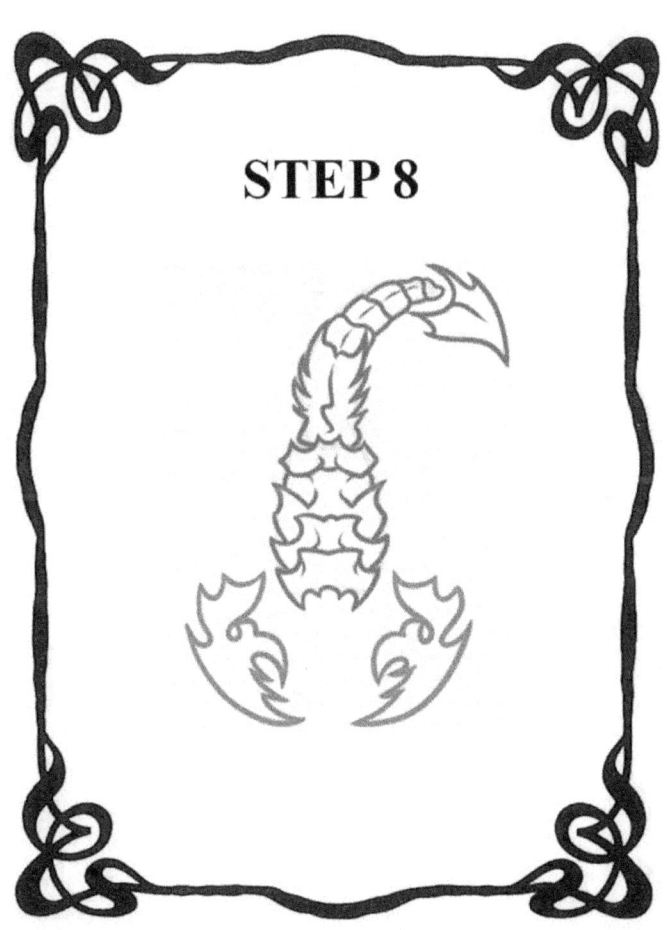

STEP 9

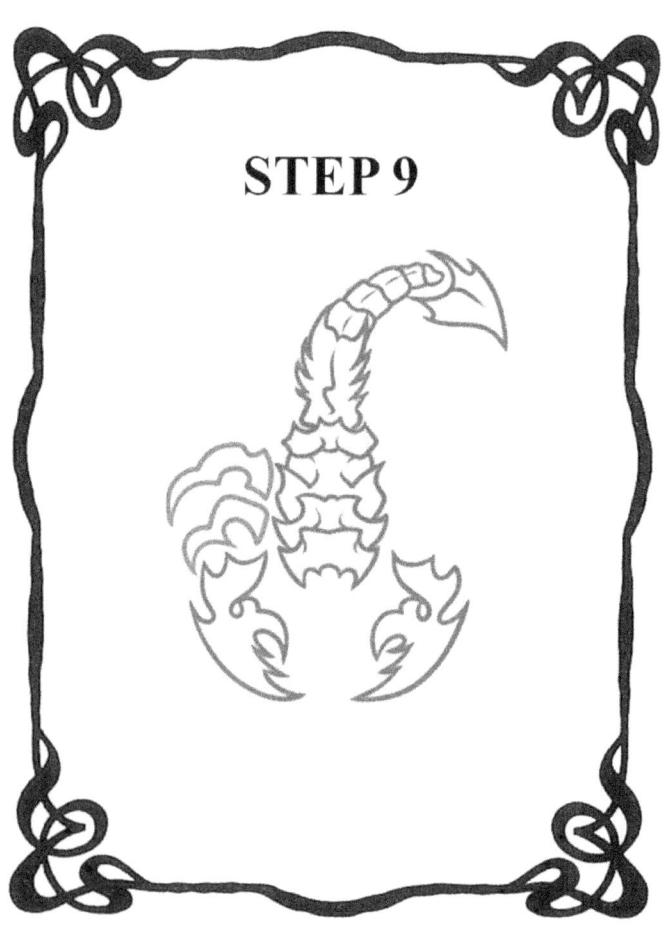

STEP 10

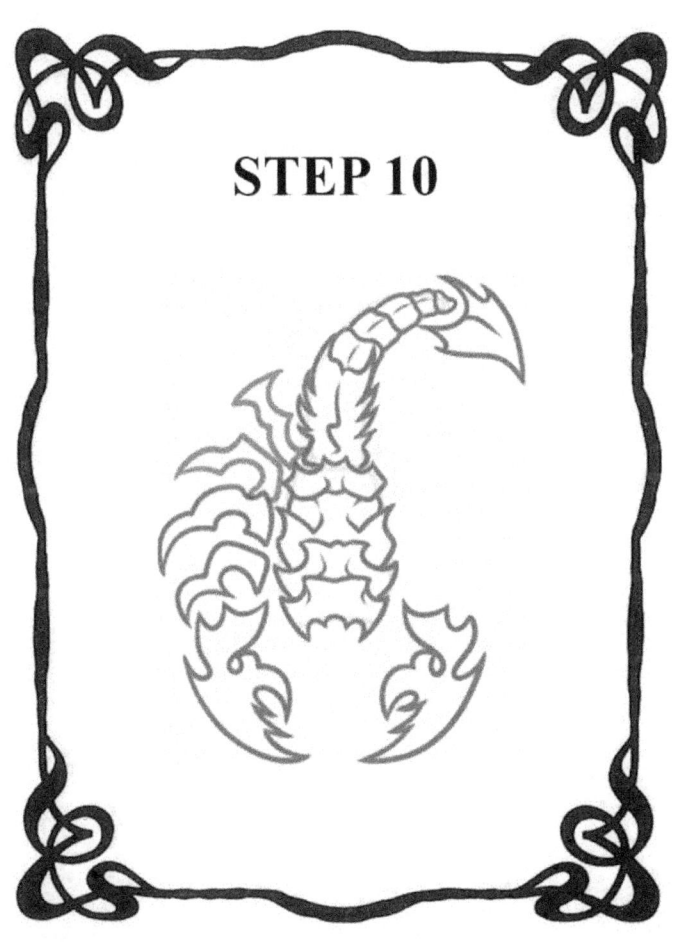

STEP 11

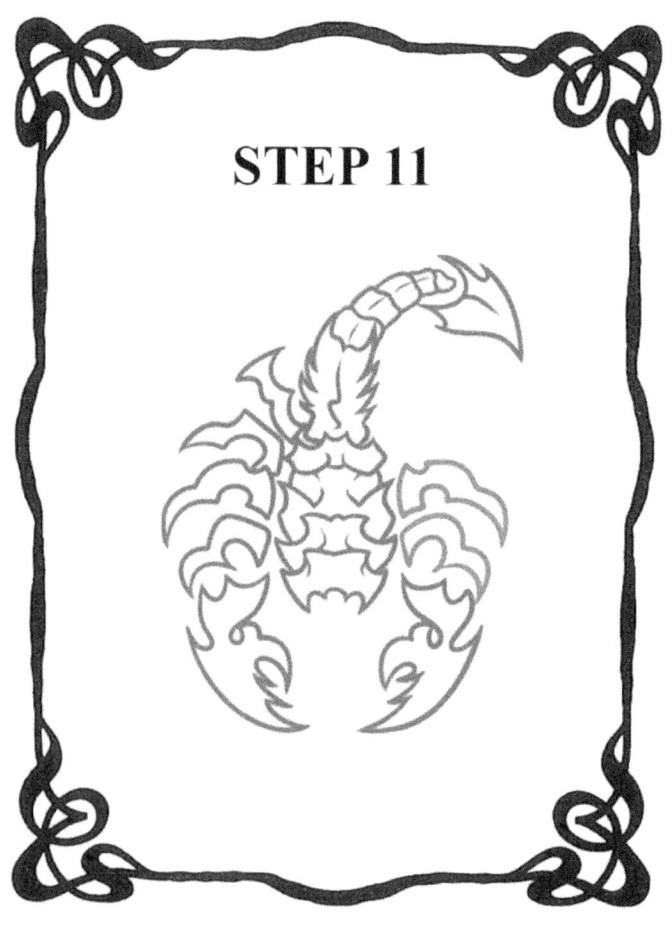

STEP 12

SHARK TATTOO

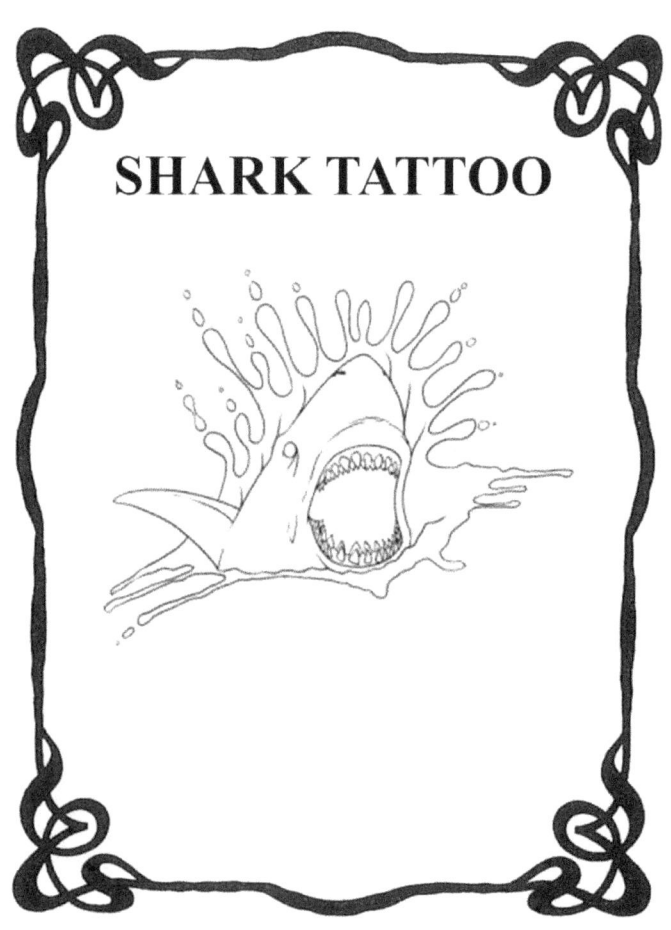

STEP 1

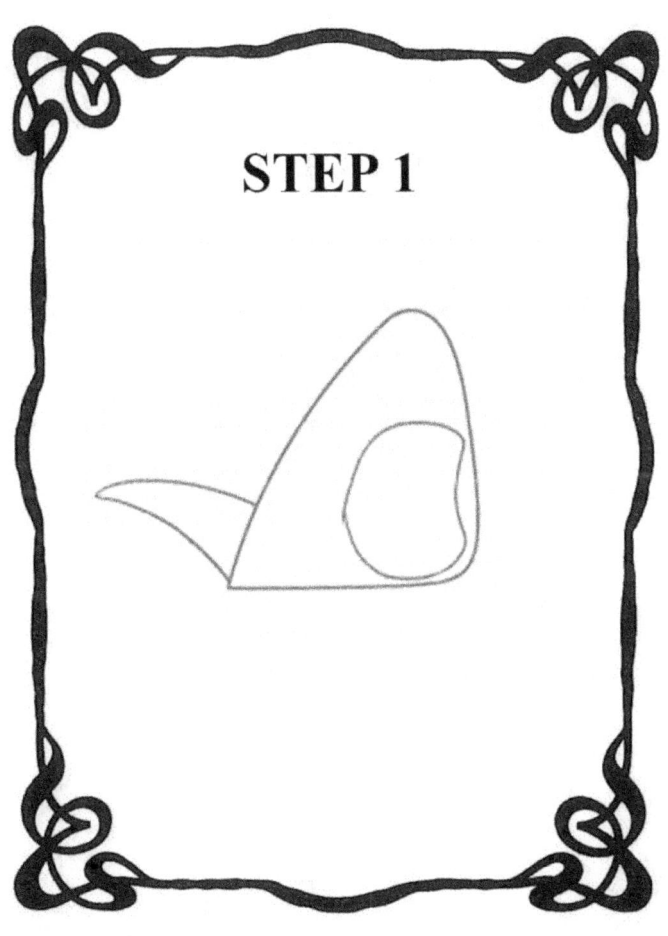

STEP 2

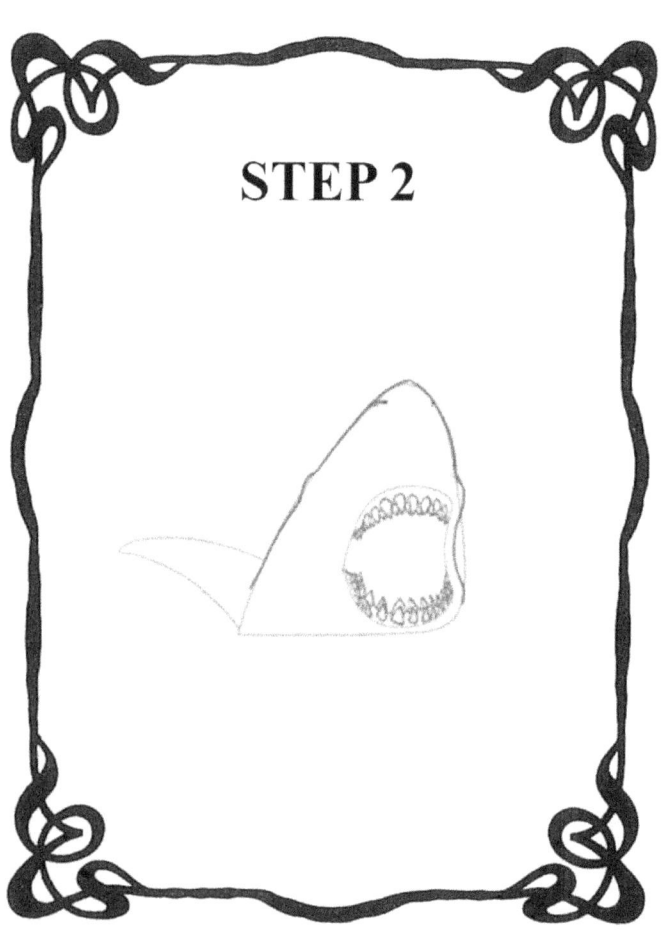

STEP 3

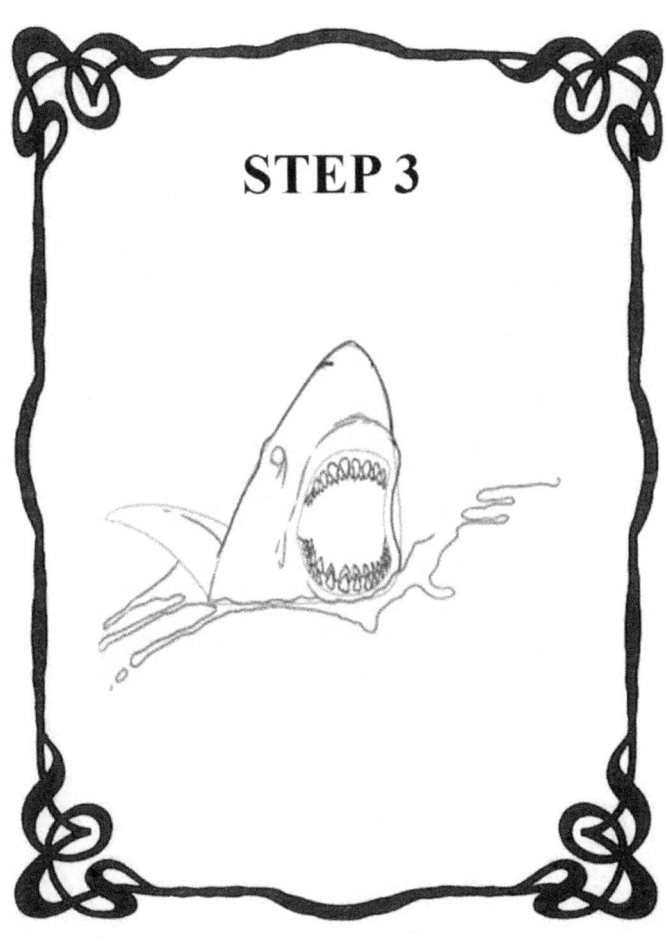

STEP 4

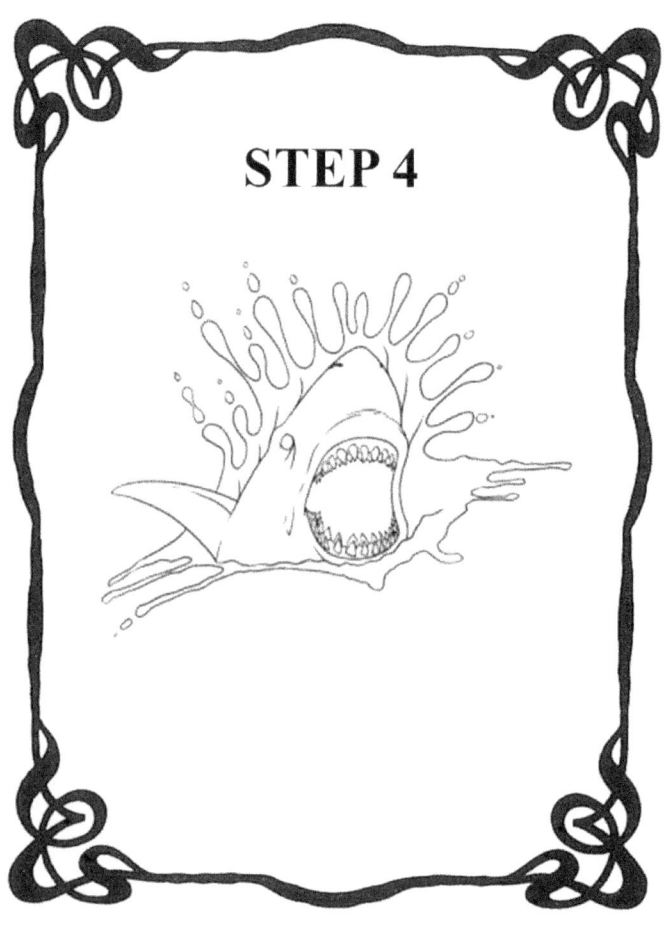

SNAKE TATTOO

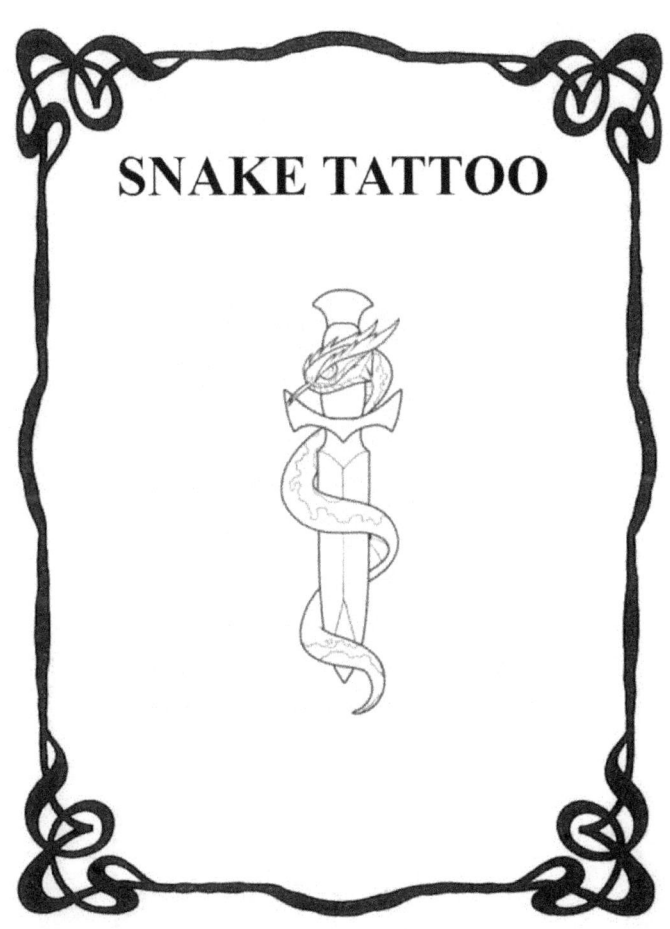

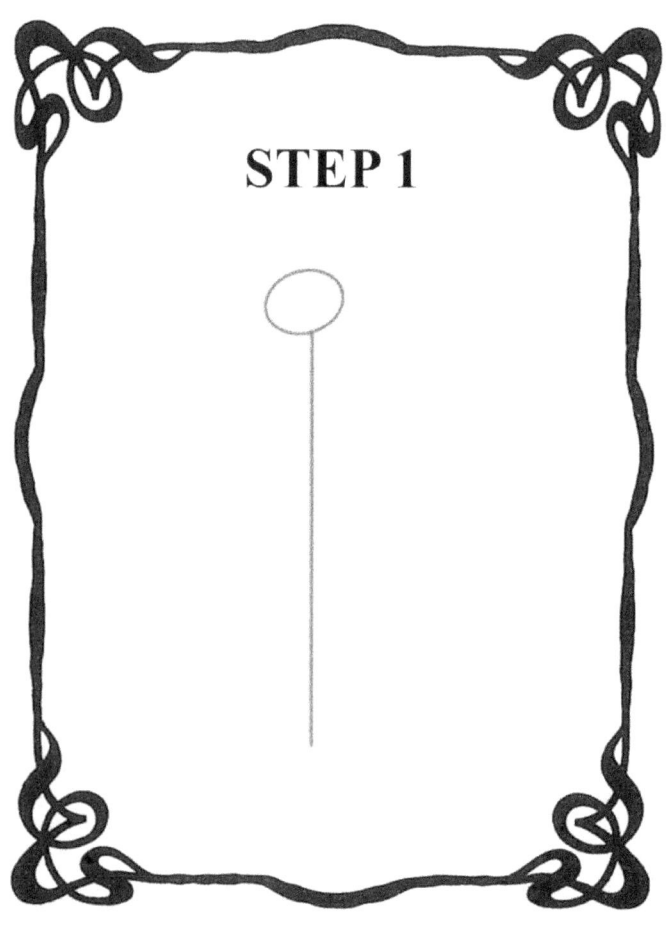

STEP 1

STEP 2

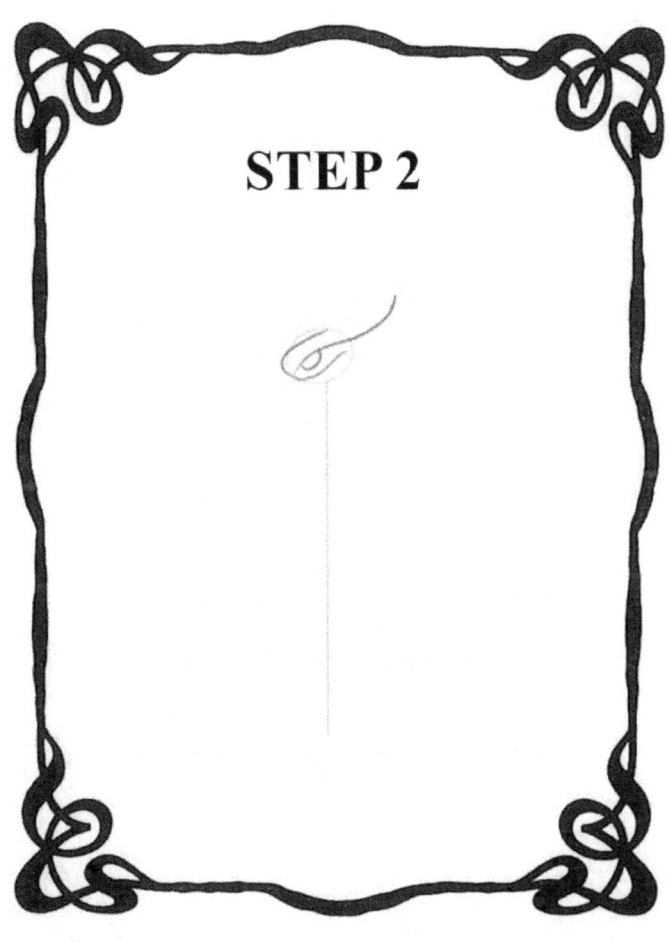

STEP 3

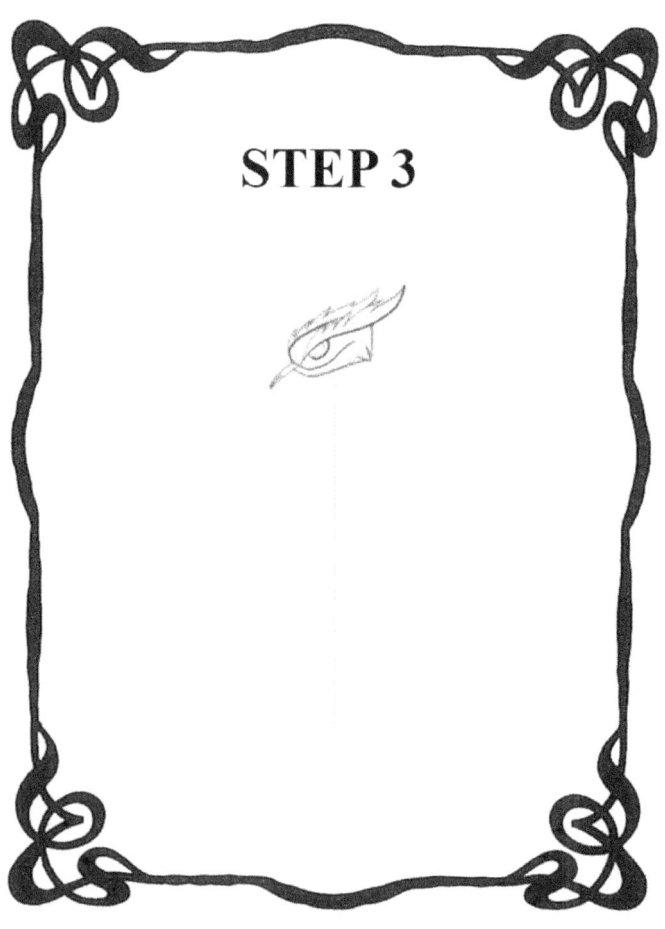

STEP 4

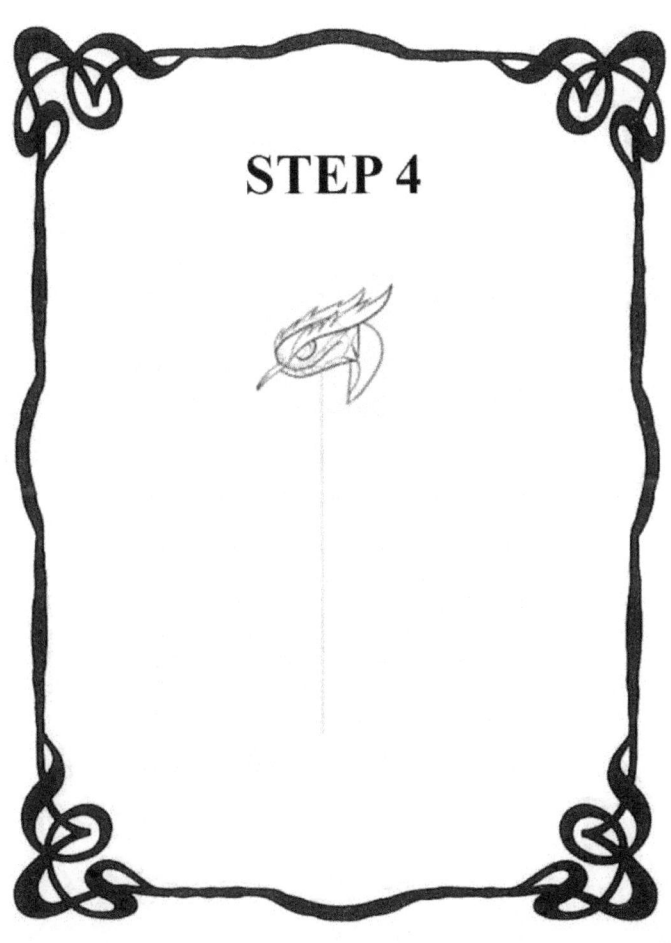

STEP 5

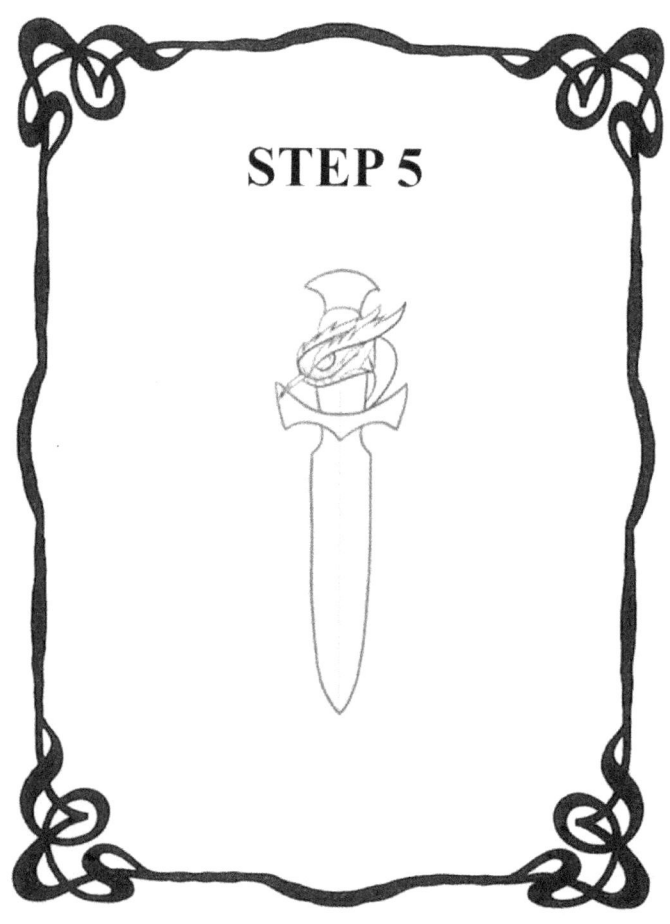

STEP 6

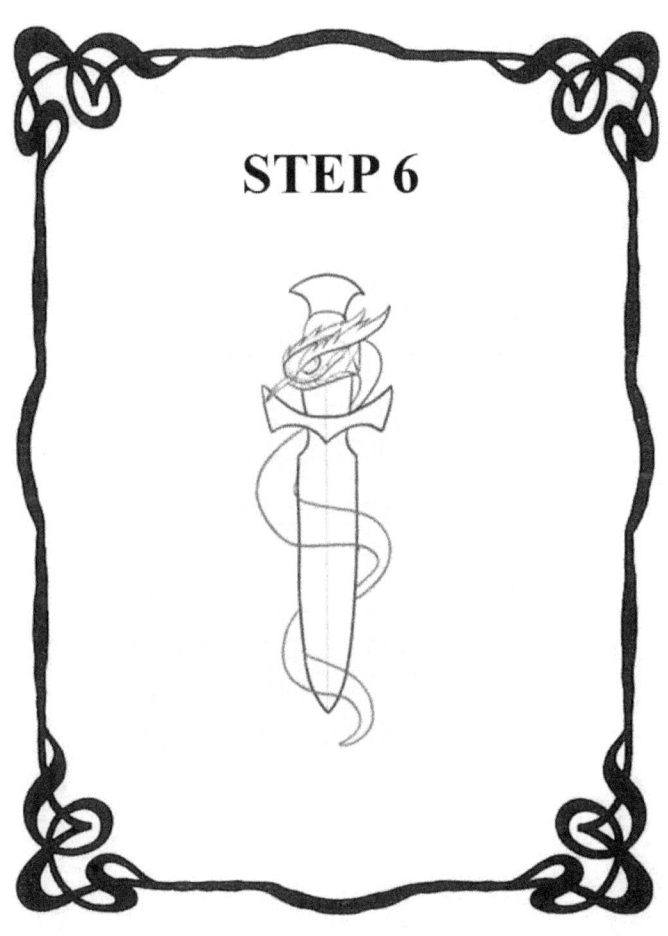

STEP 7

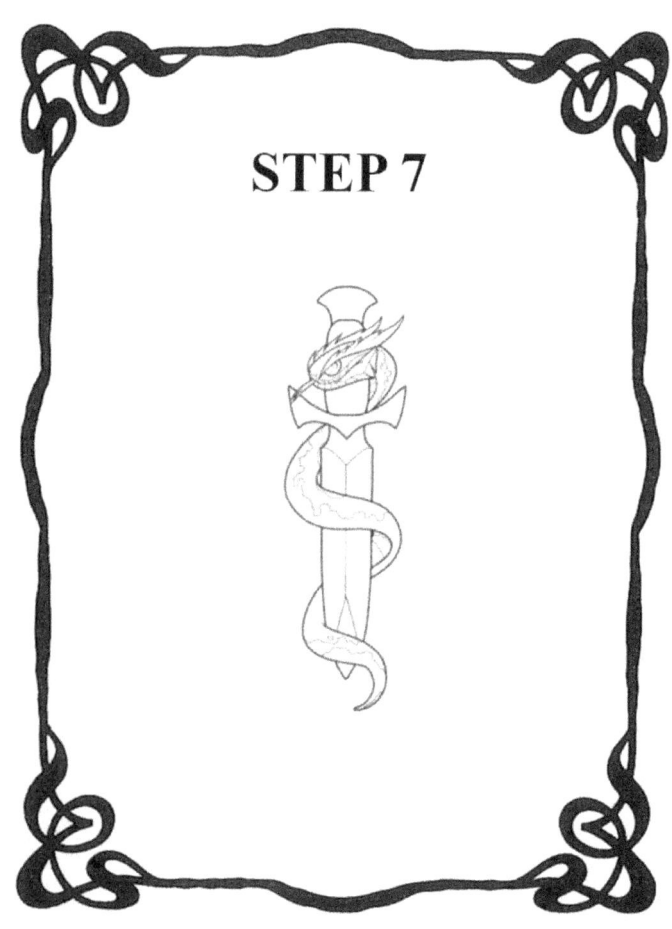

t

SPARROW TATTOO

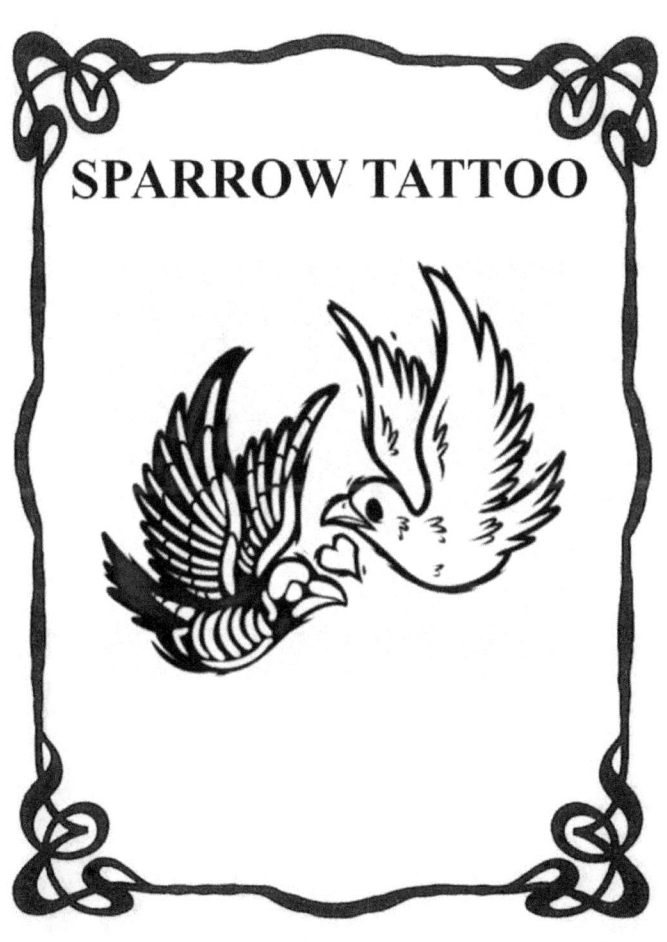

STEP 1

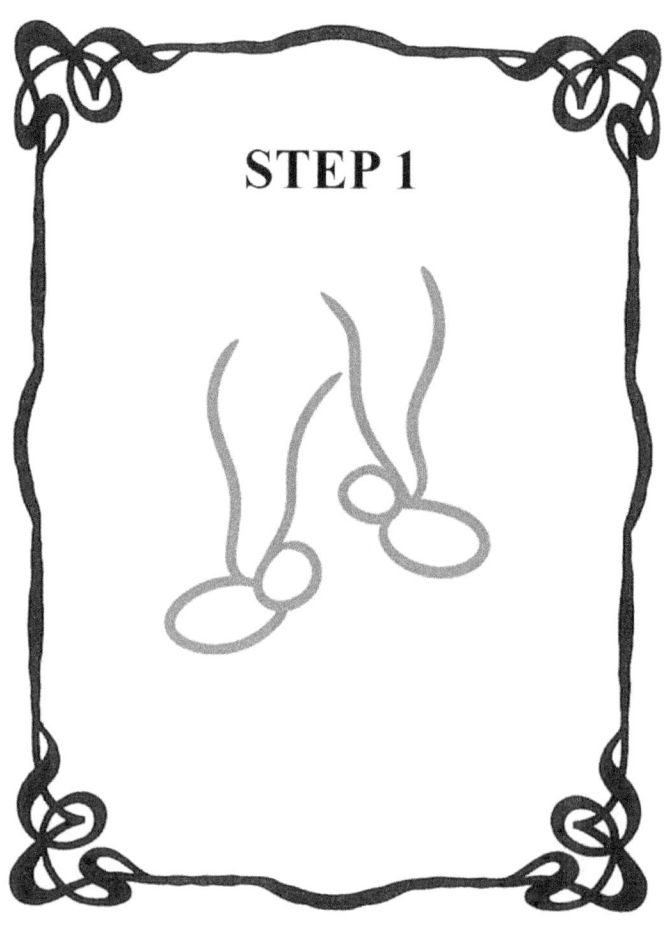

STEP 2

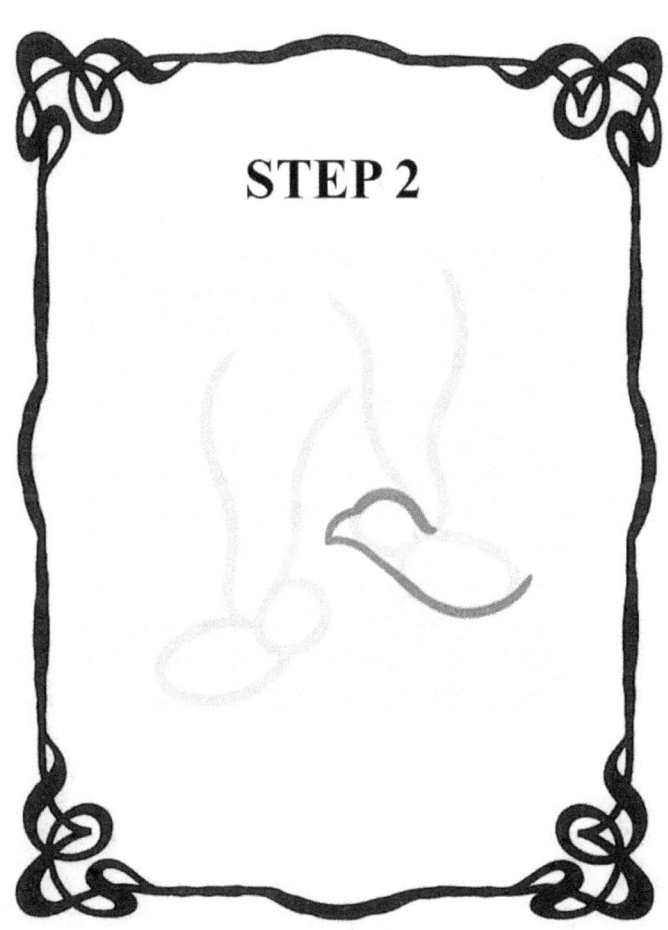

STEP 3

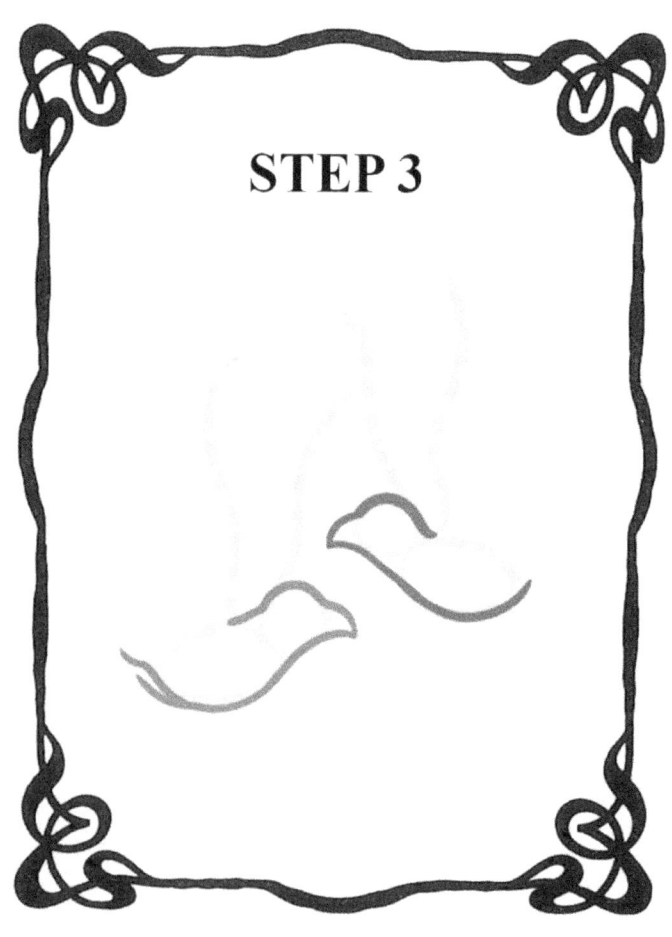

STEP 4

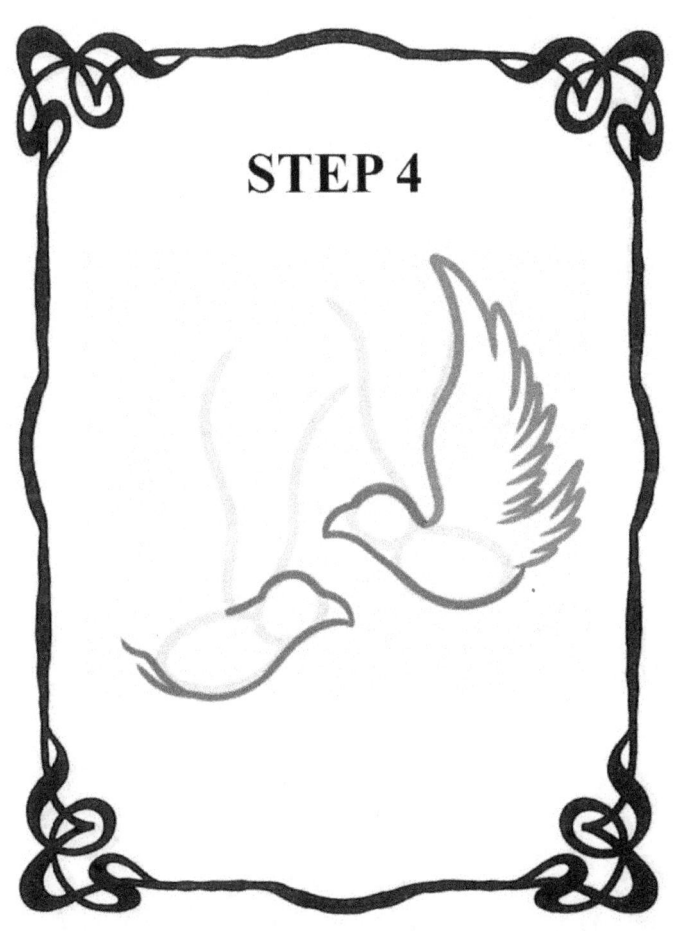

STEP 5

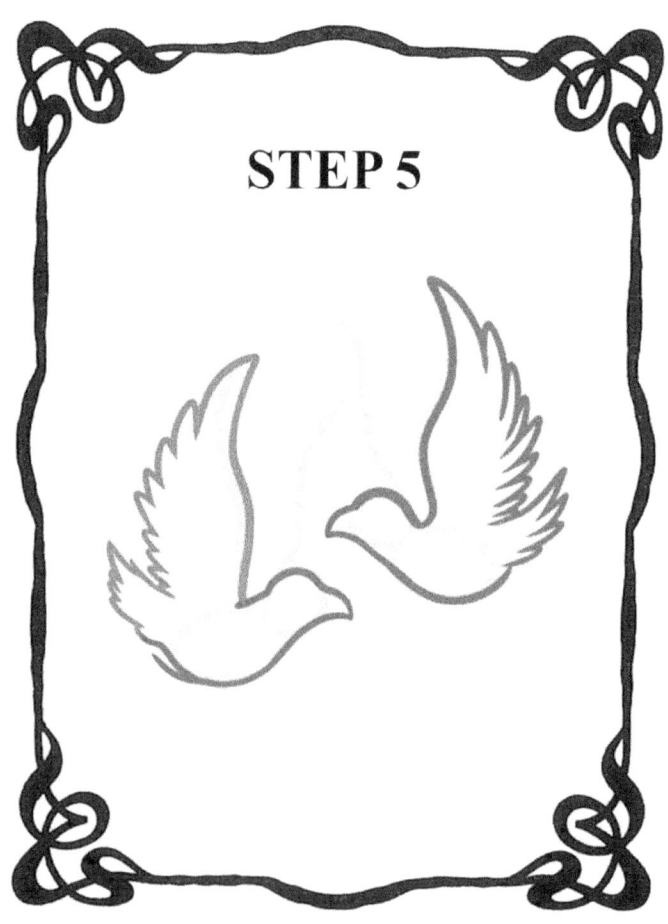

STEP 6

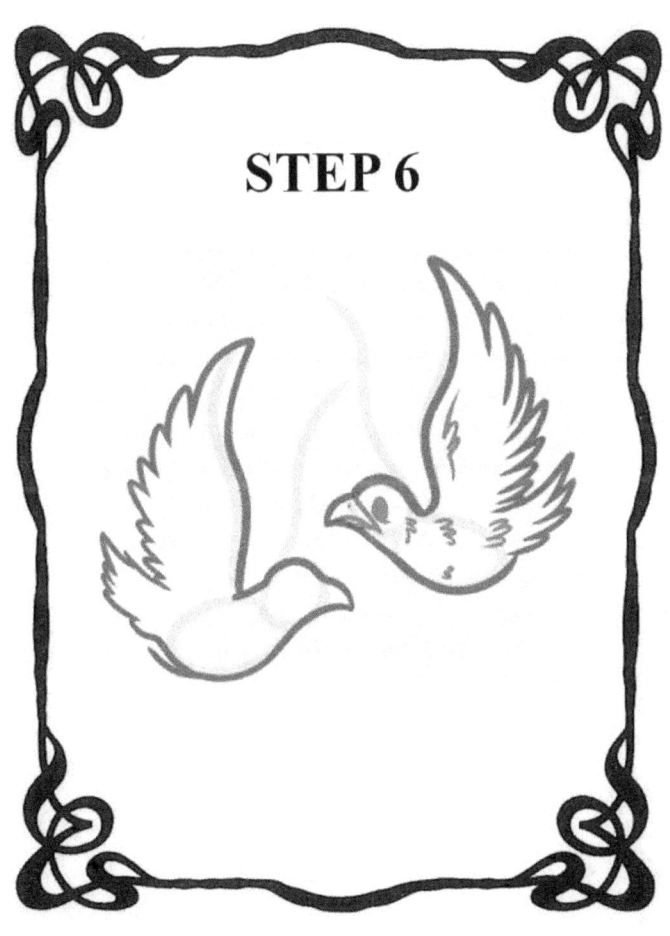

STEP 7

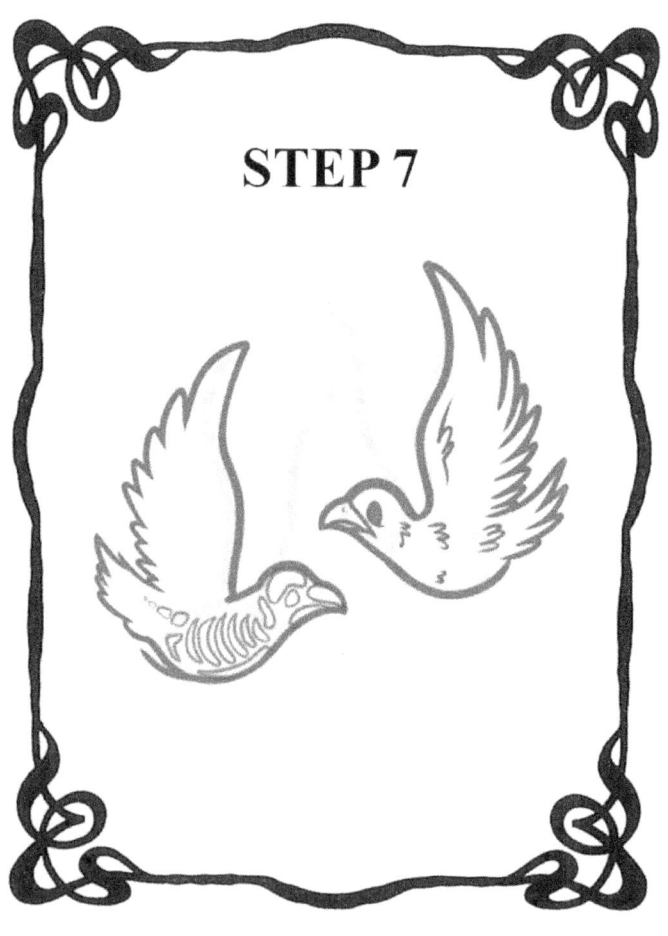

STEP 8

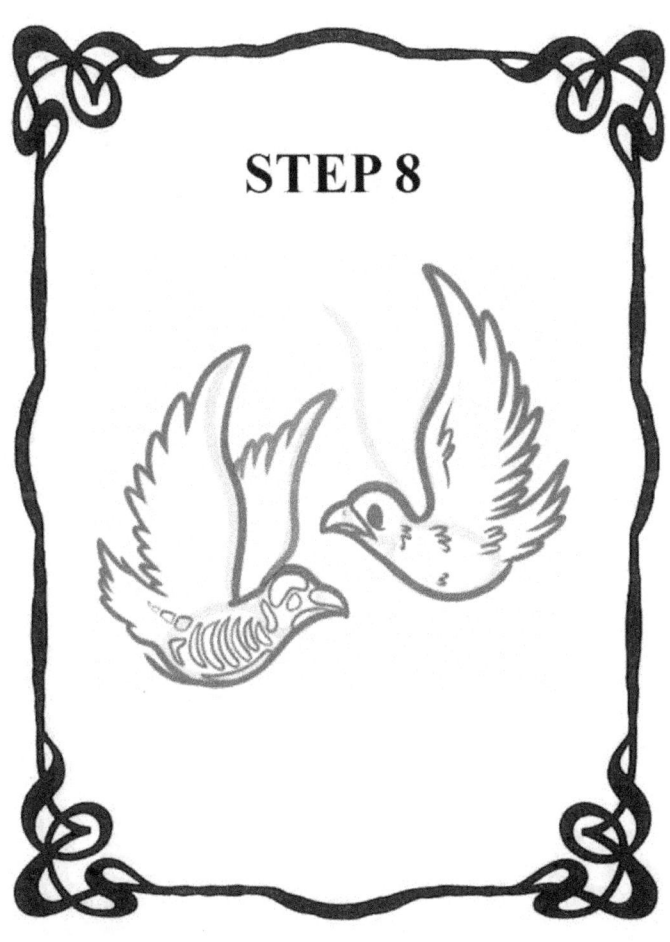

STEP 9

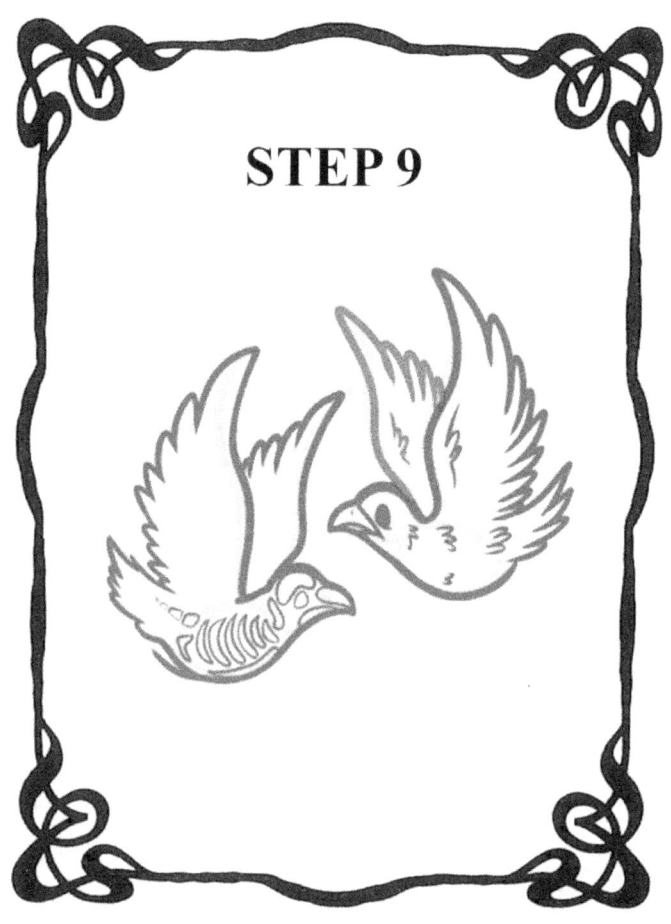

STEP 10

STEP 11

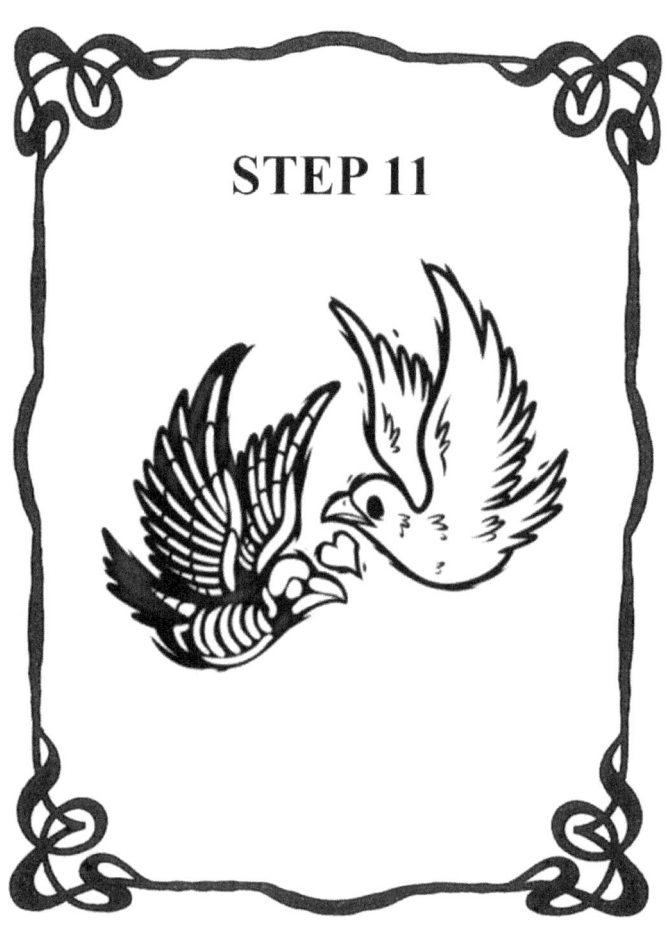

SWALLOW TATTOO

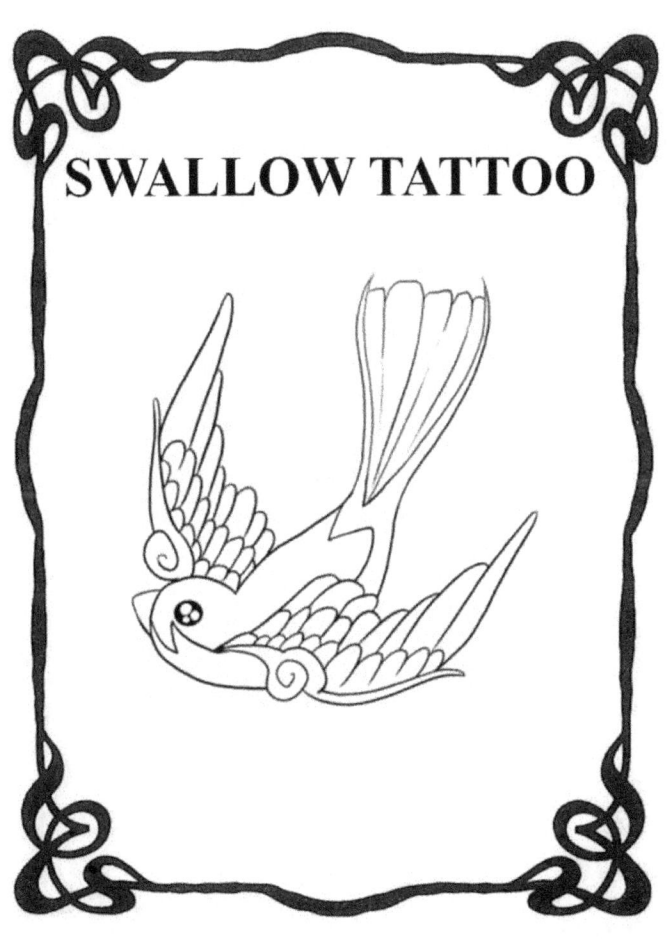

STEP 1

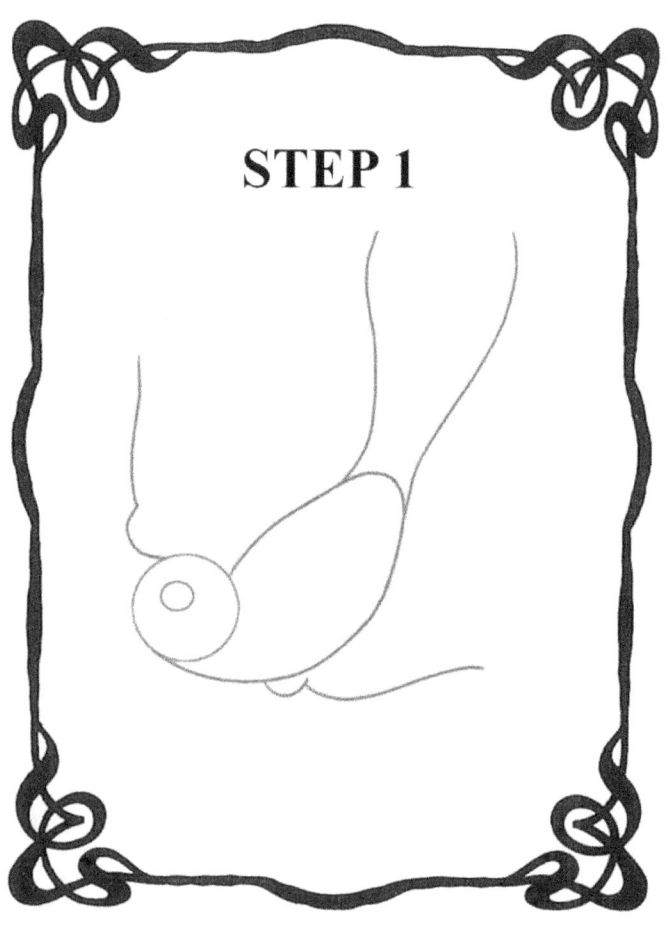

STEP 2

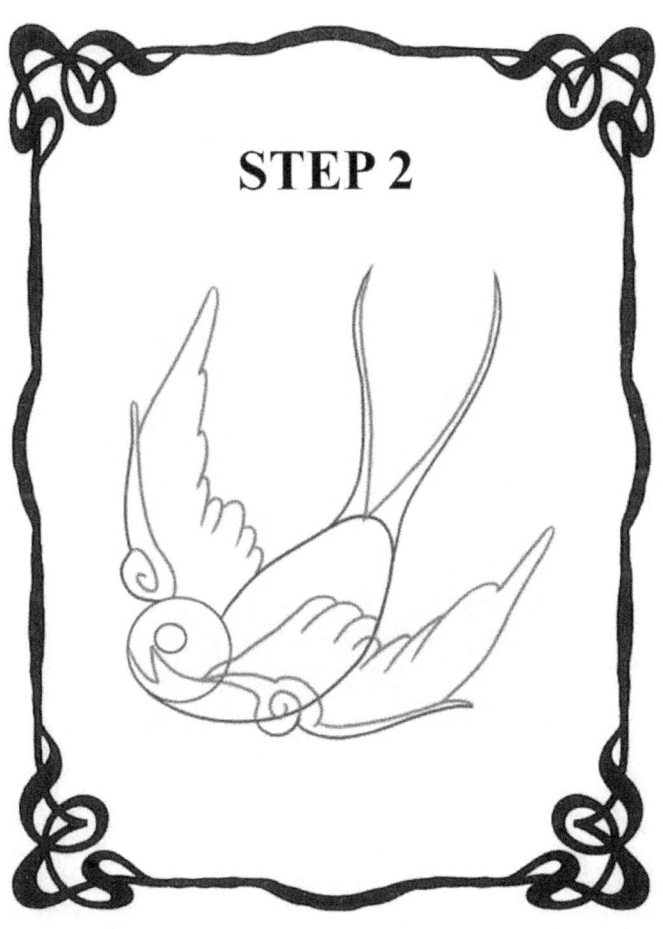

STEP 3

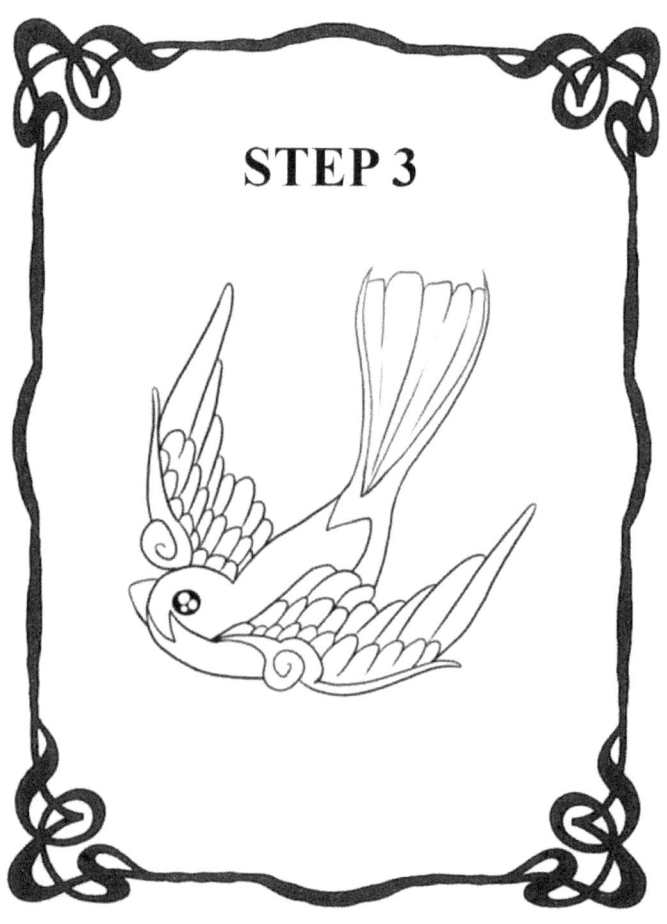

TURTLE TATTOO

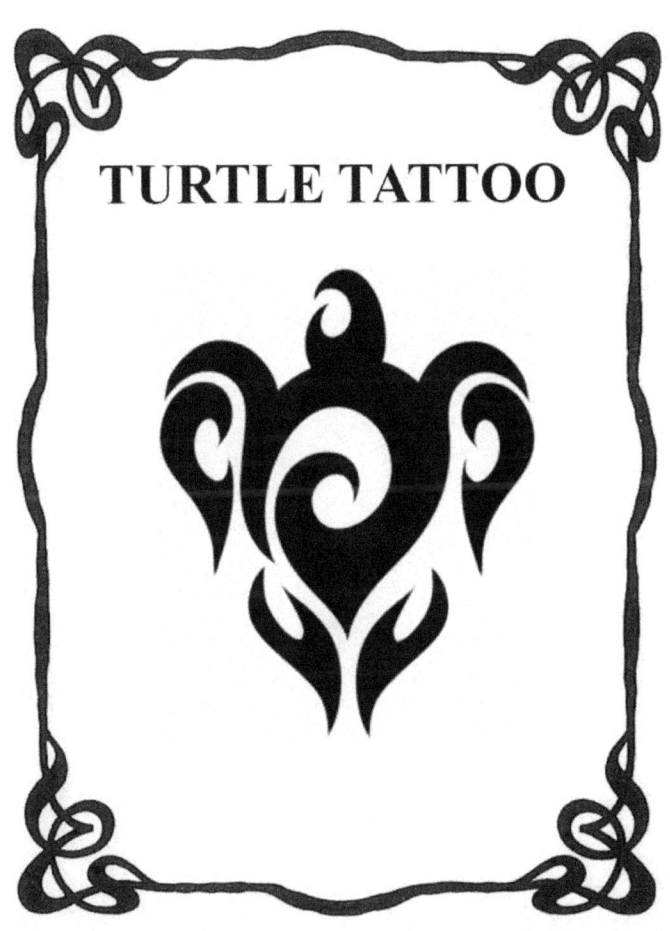

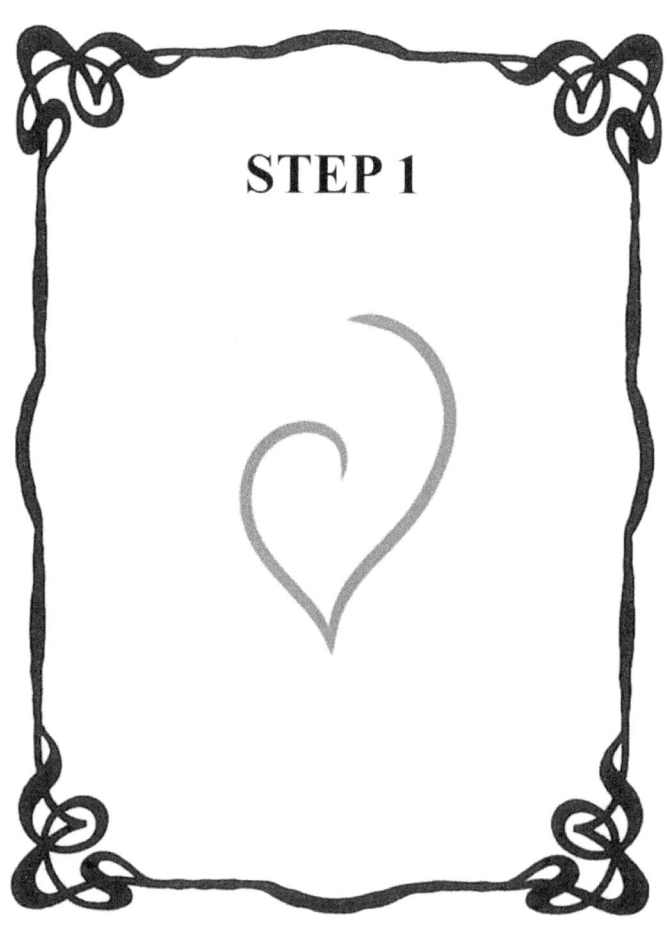

STEP 1

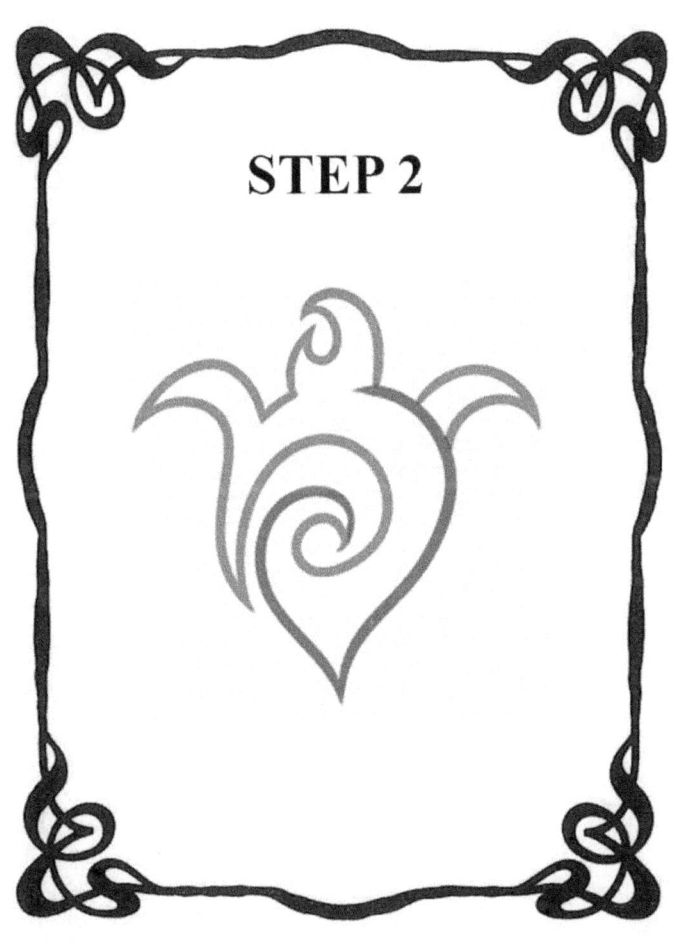

STEP 2

STEP 3

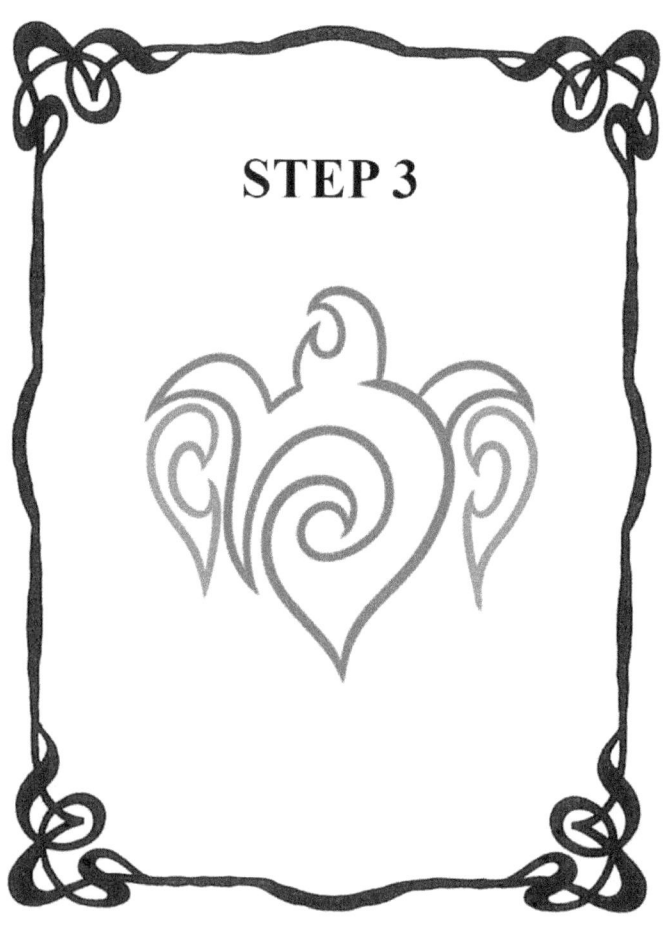

STEP 4

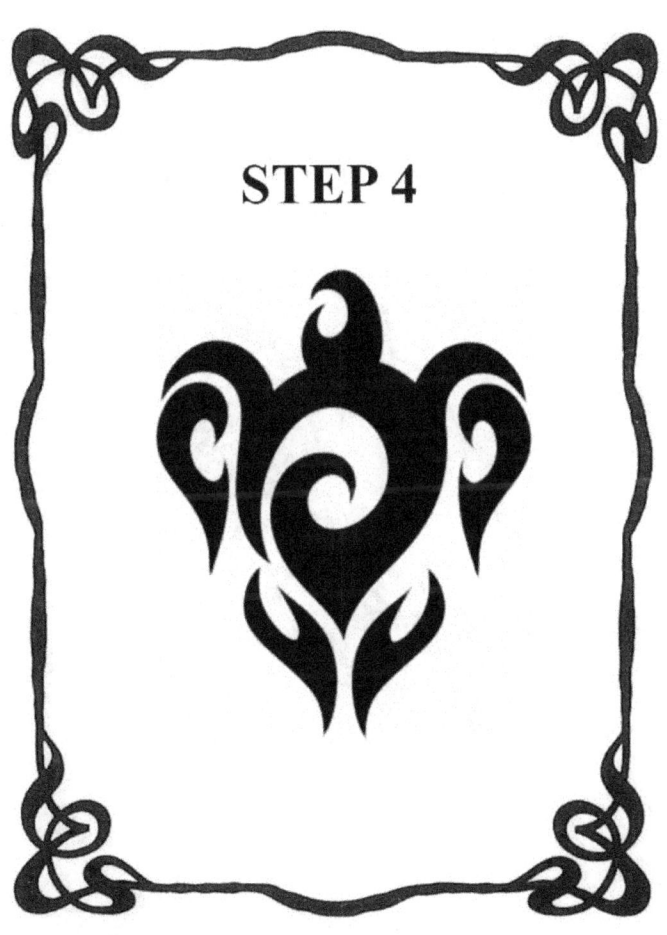

WOLF TATTOO

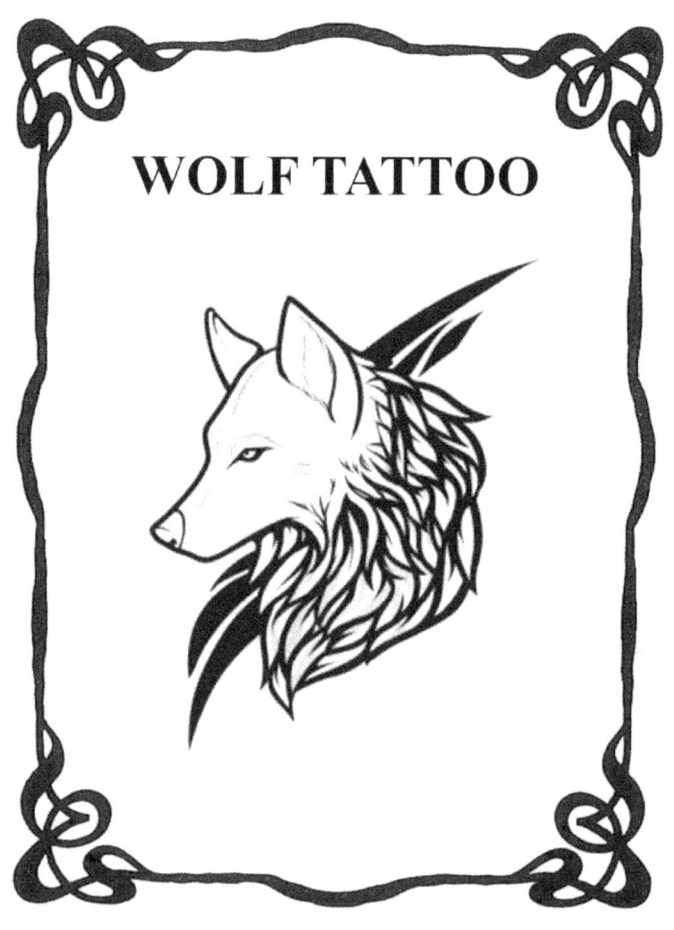

STEP 1

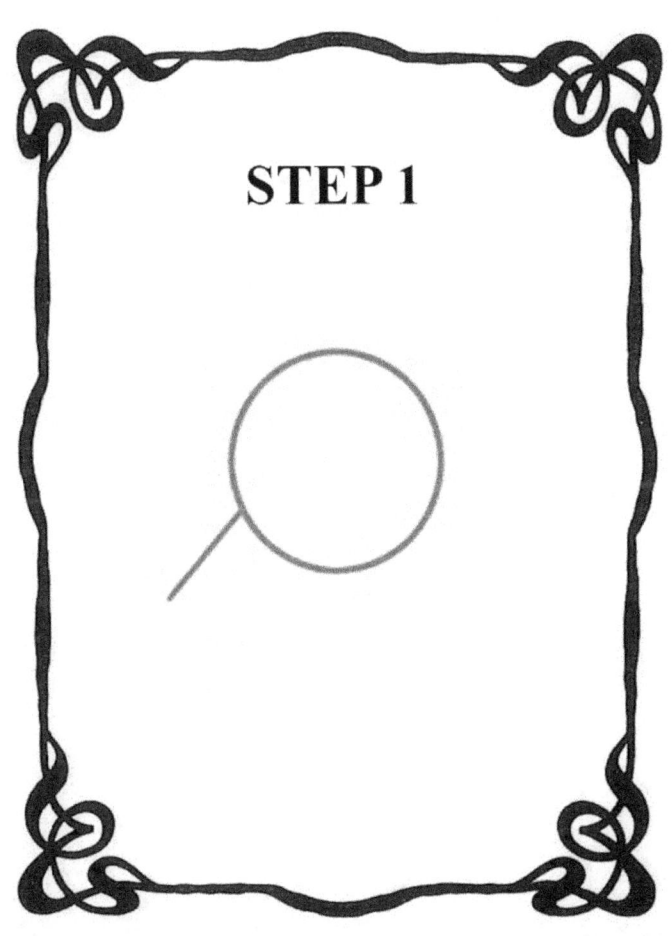

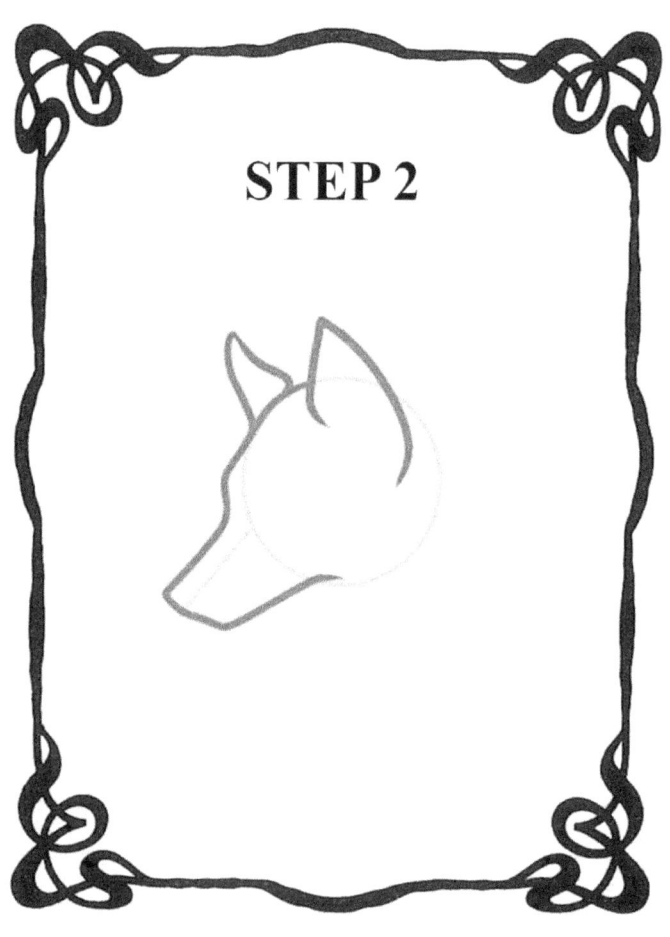

54

STEP 2

STEP 3

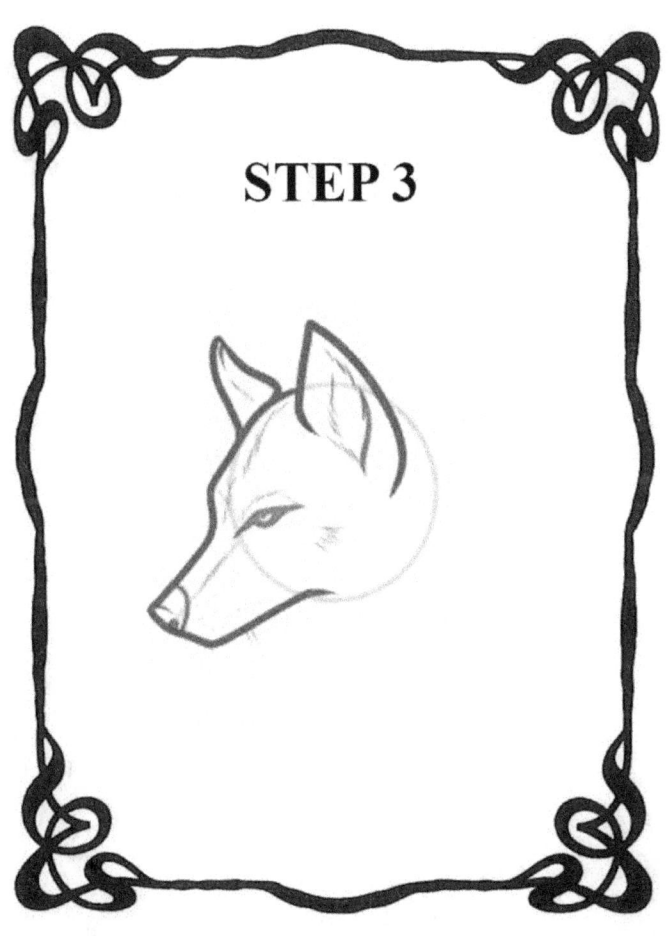

STEP 4

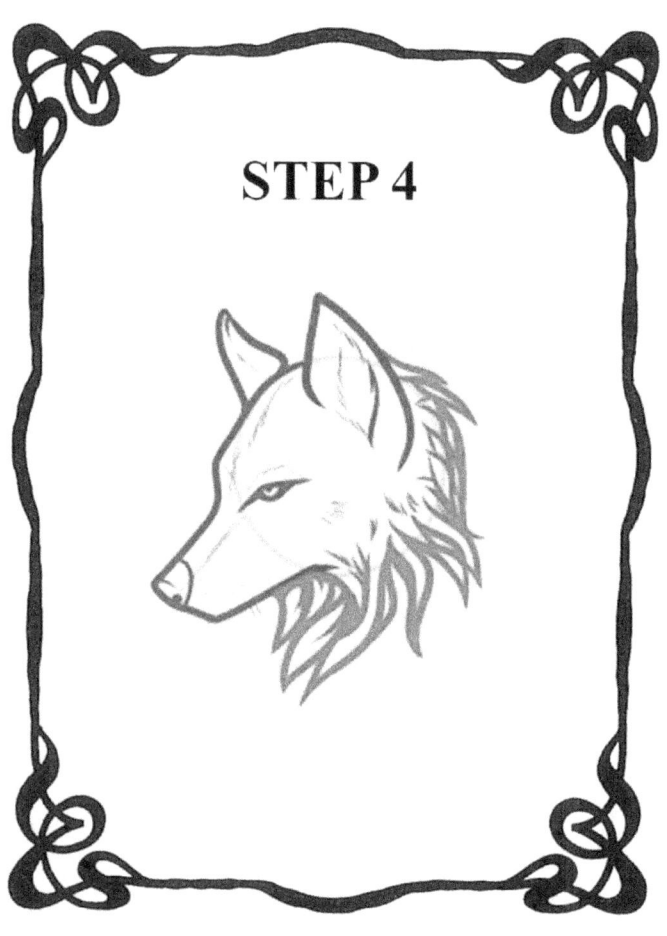

STEP 5

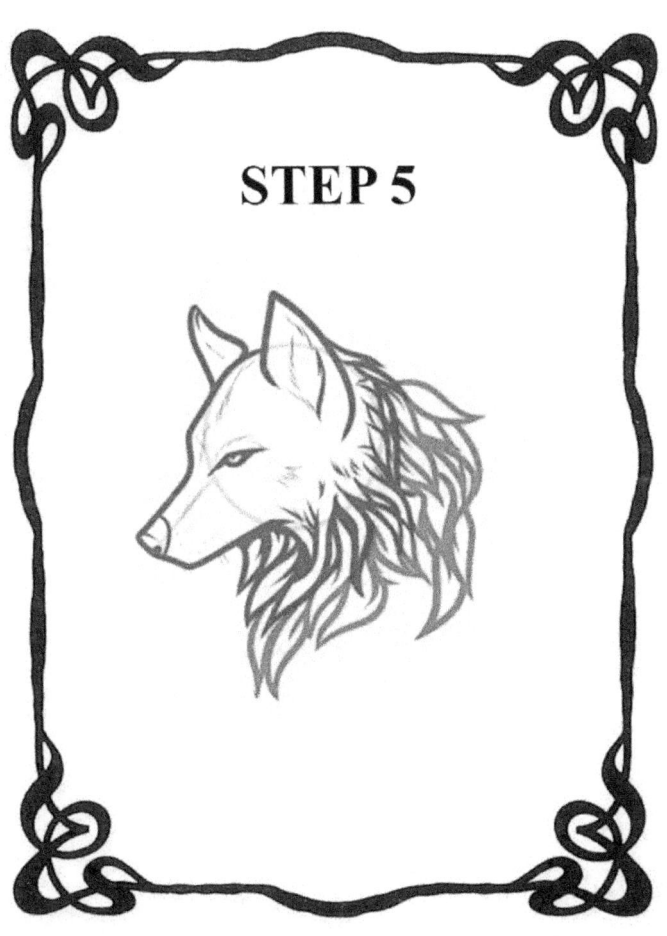

STEP 6

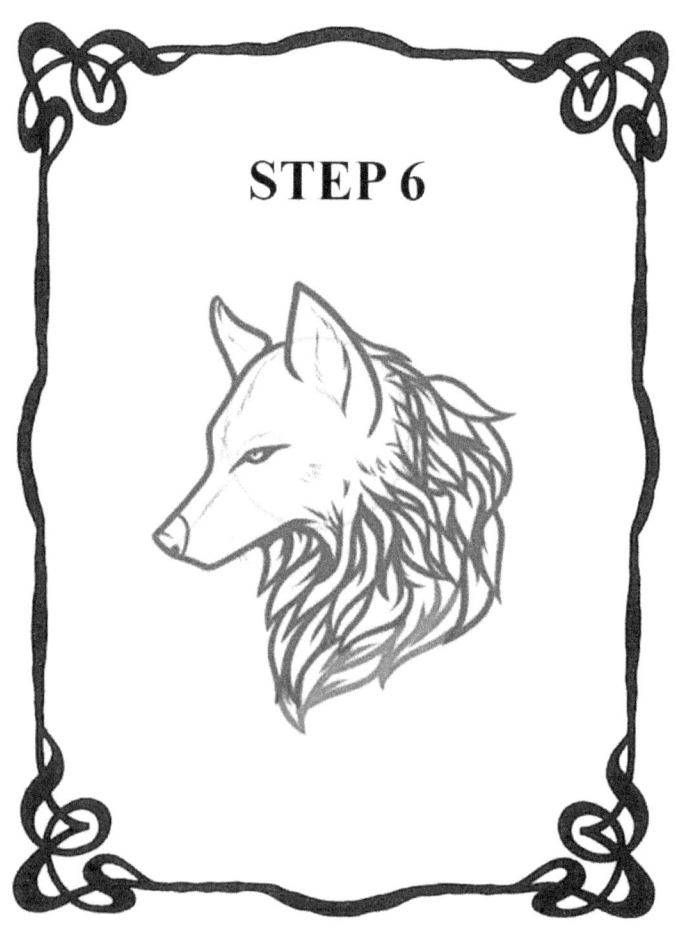

STEP 7

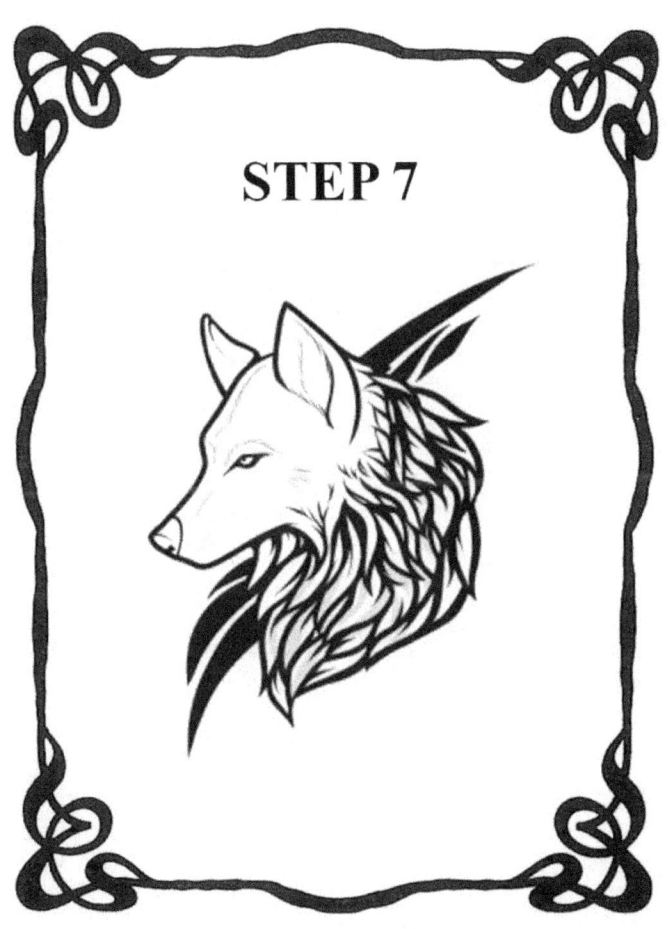

www.ingramcontent.com/pod-product-compliance
Lightning Source LLC
Chambersburg PA
CBHW071636170526
45166CB00003B/1342